Hauntings

Peter Hepplewhite ● Neil Tonge

Hamlyn Children's

Publisher: Zuza Vrbova
Editor: Richard Widdows
Art Editor: Donna Payne
Designers: Paul Webb and John Jamieson
Illustrations: Eric Rowe at Linden Artists
Picture Researcher: Suzanne Williams
Production: Christine Campbell
Cover design: Ian Butterworth

Consultant: Philip Mantle of the British UFO Research Association

069391

Picture Credits

Fortean Picture Library: page 8 (Andreas Trottman),
page 12 (Janet and Colin Bord), page 21 right;
Robert Harding Picture Library: pages 18-19 (FPG), pages 41 and 44;
Hulton Getty Pictures: page 18 bottom, page 33;
Mary Evans Picture Library: pages 16-17;
Peter Newark's Military and American Pictures: pages 20-21, page 28, page 36;
Photodisc Inc. : Cover;
Popperfoto: page 19 top.

Published in 1997 by Hamlyn Children's Books, an imprint of Reed International Books,
Michelin House, 81 Fulham Road, London SW3 6RB and Auckland and Melbourne
Illustrations © 1997 Reed International Books Limited
Text © 1997 Peter Hepplewhite & Neil Tonge.
The authors have asserted their moral rights.

ISBN 0 600 59299 5
First Edition
10 9 8 7 6 5 4 3 2 1
A CIP catalogue record for this book is available from the British Library.
Printed in Italy by Olivotto

••••••••➤ Contents

THE GHOST SOLDIERS In 1953 a young lad was working alone in an old cellar in York when he saw Roman soldiers march through solid stone walls. Nobody believed his fantastic "ghost story", but a few years later evidence was uncovered that seemed to back up his tale of a visit from the distant past.

THE DOOMED VOYAGE At the end of the 19th century a book was published that described the sinking of an "unsinkable" passenger ship. Fourteen years later, the great ocean liner *Titanic* sank to a cold grave on its maiden voyage. Both vessels were hit by an iceberg in the North Atlantic, both had too few lifeboats, both saw massive loss of life. And that's not all...

THE DREAM OF DEATH In April 1865 Abraham Lincoln, President of the USA, suffered a nightmare dream — about his own death at the hands of an assassin. Ten days later, Lincoln was shot dead on a visit to the theatre in one of the most dramatic events of American history.

THE LOST LEADER In the wartime London of 1943, a chilling telephone call to the headquarters of the Free Polish forces predicts the death in an air crash of their leader General Sikorski. Six weeks later the General died when his plane mysteriously plunged into the sea near Gibraltar.

THE PALACE OF GHOSTS On a quiet visit to the gardens of Versailles near Paris, two genteel Edwardian ladies were lured by a ghostly figure into an earlier time. Was this the vivid imagination of two women — or a "time slip" into a very different past?

Introducing more great titles in
The Unexplained series.

When it comes to the world of the supernatural and the paranormal, there's a lot to talk about. Together with *Hauntings*, these are the other brilliant books in this brand new series hot off the Hamlyn production line.

THE UNCANNY ⟩⟩

Funny goings-on in mind, body and spirit

⟨⟨ MYSTERIOUS PLACES

Strange happenings in remote regions

ALIEN ⟩⟩
ENCOUNTERS

Close connections of the extra-terrestrial kind

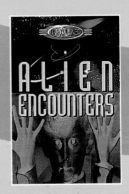

Hauntings

Have you ever seen a ghost, or had the feeling that you knew exactly what was going to happen? Many reliable witnesses claim to have "slipped" into different time zones peopled by ghosts of the past and spectres of the future. Chilling sights have been seen and terrible warnings have been received.

The human mind is a force of great power and imagination. But is it powerful enough to break free of the present and witness events from another era? Or is it simply imaginative enough to invent such vivid experiences, triggered by strong emotions? *Hauntings* features five famous "time slips" and explores the theories that may help to explain them.

When you read about ghostly goings-on, you need an open mind. Nonsense or common sense? The Unexplained series lets YOU decide what to believe . . .

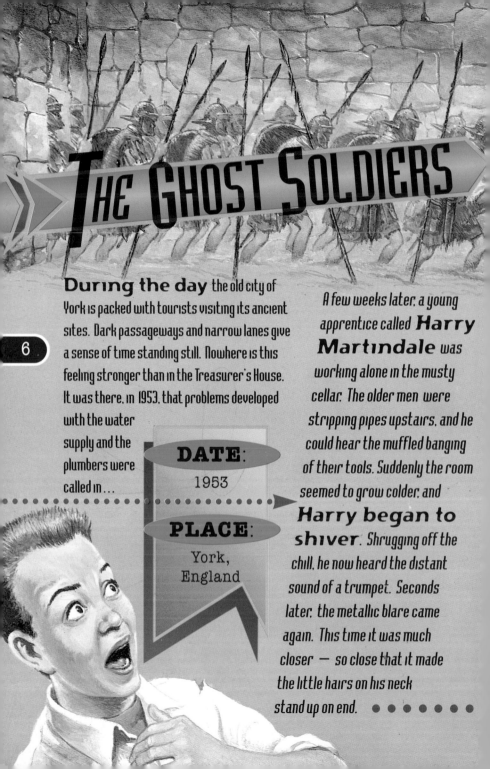

THE GHOST SOLDIERS

During the day the old city of York is packed with tourists visiting its ancient sites. Dark passageways and narrow lanes give a sense of time standing still. Nowhere is this feeling stronger than in the Treasurer's House. It was there, in 1953, that problems developed with the water supply and the plumbers were called in ...

DATE: 1953

PLACE: York, England

A few weeks later, a young apprentice called **Harry Martindale** was working alone in the musty cellar. The older men were stripping pipes upstairs, and he could hear the muffled banging of their tools. Suddenly the room seemed to grow colder, and **Harry began to shiver**. Shrugging off the chill, he now heard the distant sound of a trumpet. Seconds later, the metallic blare came again. This time it was much closer — so close that it made the little hairs on his neck stand up on end.

Without warning, the head of a pony loomed out of the thick cellar wall. Harry staggered back in shock. Impossible as it seemed, the rest of the animal slowly followed. It was tired and ragged-looking, wearily plodding along with a rider on its back. Close behind came 14 or maybe 16 infantrymen, walking in double file. They were trailing their spears on the ground, their heads hanging low. It looked as if they were near the end of their strength after a long, desperate march.

Sweat had left streaks on their dusty faces. A thin veil of powdery dirt covered their leather uniforms, and their weapons were black with neglect. The soldiers all wore short, green kilts, and they had leather helmets. The mounted man had a red plume in his helmet, and he wore an old cloak that trailed along the flanks of his pony.

He watched OPEN-MOUTHED...

Harry cowered in the corner, hoping that the shadows hid him as the soldiers straggled past. He watched open-mouthed as they trailed across the cellar behind their officer — and out through the opposite wall! They looked strangely small, until Harry realised that their feet were hidden from view. When they reached a hole dug in the cellar, their ankles and feet briefly appeared. He then saw their leather sandals, tied on with long thongs criss-crossing up their tired legs.

Treasurer's House, York

WITNESS

Harry Martindale thought of himself as being reliable and level-headed. He later became a policeman.

As the last figure vanished through the wall, Harry made a desperate run for the stairs, bounding up them two at a time. Gasping, he blurted out his amazing news to his workmates. "The young lad's spooked," they laughed. "He's been alone in that cellar too long!"

Harry put up with their jokes, but he stuck to his story. And a few years later, evidence was uncovered that made his friends think again…

SUPPORTING WITNESSES

In 1960, <u>two</u> archaeologists working in the same cellar reported an **identical sighting** of Roman soldiers…

"The young lad's spooked. He's been alone in that cellar too long!"

HAUNTING EVIDENCE

...A ROMAN ROAD BELOW THE CELLAR FLOOR.

A strong point in favour of Harry's story is that he could not see the soldiers' ankles. Archaeologists exploring the site later found the remains of a Roman road about 35 centimetres below the cellar floor. The Treasurer's House lay across one of the main routes into the fort at York. The Roman soldiers had been walking in exactly the right place for their time!

Harry had a good eye for detail. He noticed that the soldiers carried circular shields and different weapons, from short swords to long spears. At first, this seemed to suggest that his story _was_ invented, because Roman soldiers carried long, body-hugging shields. But historians pointed out that Harry could have seen Roman _auxiliary_ soldiers. These were support troops from places in the Roman Empire, and they often continued to use the weapons of their homelands. Such units were stationed at York — and carried round shields.

HAUNTING ANSWERS

THEORY 1 - FEAR!

Harry could have imagined his "haunting", perhaps frightened by working on his own in the old cellar.

THEORY 2 - A TIME RECORDING

A second explanation is that Harry saw a replay of a past event. Some researchers believe that when people experience strong emotions, their feelings are "imprinted" on buildings or the landscape, much like a video recording. Could Harry have witnessed an action replay of beaten Romans retreating to the safety of the fortress at York?

Infant Sacrifice at Reculver?

For many years the sound of a crying baby has disturbed visitors to the Roman fort at Reculver, on the north Kent coast of England. Local legend told stories of Romans sacrificing babies there — and when archaeologists explored the site, they discovered the skeletons of 11 young children. Most of the burials appeared to be normal, and have been dated after the Romans left. However, bones of one child were found buried in the foundations of the fort wall, and bones of a second were in the rubble core of the wall itself.

The Mystery of the Ninth Legion

The Ninth Legion of the Roman Army was stationed at York, but no trace of them can be found in surviving records after 108 AD. So what happened to them?
The records of a legion were usually destroyed if it had deserted in battle or mutinied. Some historians believe the Ninth was almost wiped out in a battle in Scotland. Could Harry have seen the broken remnants of the Ninth Legion, and the auxiliary units fighting alongside them, staggering back from defeat north of Hadrian's Wall?

"BEWARE THE IDES OF MARCH!"

Julius Caesar was made Emperor of Rome in February 44 BC. A month later he was murdered! But he had been warned. The priest Spurinna told him to beware of danger until the Ides of March — **the 15th day of the month.** Caesar ignored his advice, and on the morning of his death he met the priest. "The Ides of March have come, and I am unharmed," he boasted. "Yes, they have come," replied the priest, "but they have not yet gone!" Within minutes Caesar was dead, **stabbed 23 times.**

Perhaps Caesar should have known better...

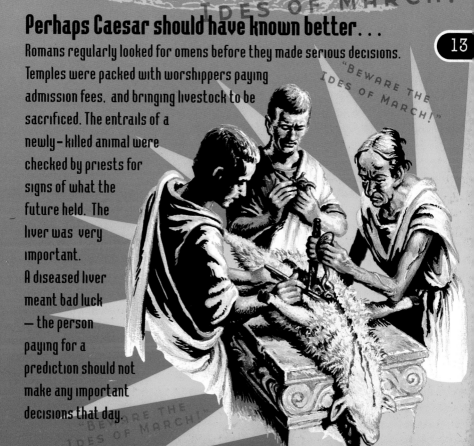

Romans regularly looked for omens before they made serious decisions. Temples were packed with worshippers paying admission fees, and bringing livestock to be sacrificed. The entrails of a newly-killed animal were checked by priests for signs of what the future held. The liver was very important. A diseased liver meant bad luck — the person paying for a prediction should not make any important decisions that day.

THE DOOMED VOYAGE

Her owners boasted

DATE:
15 April 1912

PLACE:
off Cape Race,
Newfoundland

that the mighty *Titanic* was "the ship that could not sink". But on a cold spring night her great steel plates were ripped apart by fangs of ice. In less than three hours she had vanished beneath the waves of the Atlantic.

Fourteen years earlier, back in 1898, the novel *Futility* predicted just such a disaster. The story, by American writer Morgan Robertson, told of a great ocean liner sunk by an iceberg. The details he described were uncannily close to the real, tragic event. Had Robertson caught a glimpse of it through the curtains of time?

Robertson's Fantasy

In Robertson's book, the ship is a huge ocean-going liner, 275 metres long and weighing 70,000 tonnes. She is a new vessel, with "state of the art", watertight compartments to make her unsinkable.

Her name? The *Titan*.

The *Titan* leaves New York in April, with 3,000 passengers and crew on board. In a North Atlantic icefield, near Cape Race, she hits a huge iceberg at a speed of 25 "knots" (about 40 kilometres an hour). She rears up over the massive obstacle, keels over and sinks quickly. The *Titan* has only 24 lifeboats on board — far too few to carry everyone — and only 13 people survive the horrific fictional disaster.

●●●●●●●●●●●●●

Morgan Robertson was a retired American seaman living in New York, trying to make a living from writing. His novel *Futility* did not sell well until 1912, when it was suddenly hailed as an astonishing prophecy of the real thing: the *Titanic* disaster.

THE REALITY

...the "safest s afloat", the Tita was claimed to "unsinkabl

*T*he *Titanic* was the pride of the White Star shipping line. This British company had been owned by the American millionaire J. P. Morgan since 1902. The *Titanic* was built in Belfast and measured 270 metres from bow to stern. She weighed over 46,000 tonnes and her engines could develop 56,000 horsepower, giving a top speed of over 40 kilometres an hour. With 16 "watertight" compartments, she was claimed to be the "safest ship afloat".

10 April 1912: the *Titanic* left the English port of Southampton, bound for New York on her maiden voyage. She was carrying 2,207 passengers and crew. Five days later, the great liner was travelling at 22 knots (about 35 km/h) in a calm, flat sea off Cape Race. Around 11.40 p.m. she struck a

towering iceberg, which ripped open her hull and six of her watertight compartments. The *Titanic* began to sink. One by one, her 20 lifeboats were launched — but there was not enough room for everyone. Women and children were given the first places in the boats, with the men taking their chances in the bitterly cold sea. At 2.10 a.m. the *Titanic* sank from sight. When the first rescue ship arrived at dawn, there were just 703 survivors.

CHALLENGING FATE

The new *Titanic* was big news in 1912. It was big—placed upright it would have been taller than any building of the day—and it was luxurious. Rich passengers could enjoy the delights of the Parisian café, the Jacobean dining-room, the tea terrace or ballroom, spaced over ten decks. Yet as soon as news of the catastrophe broke, people began saying that she had been "doomed from the start". Looking back, the claim that the *Titanic* was "unsinkable" seemed to be challenging fate.

A ship "doomed from the start"

17

Lying nearly 4,000 metres beneath the Atlantic waves, the huge hulk of the *Titanic* was investigated by the mini-submarine *Alvin* in 1986. The great ship had split into two sections as it sank, and these were found 600 metres apart on the seabed.

HAUNTING ANSWERS

THEORY 1 - SUPERNATURAL HELP

Some experts claim that Morgan Robertson had a strange dream, or fell into a trance, and then saw a vision of a great liner colliding with an iceberg. Inspired by this, he wrote his book *Futility*. There are uncanny similarities between his story and the real event, both big and small. Could he have foreseen the future?

THEORY 2 - PURE COINCIDENCE

Robertson knew about ships, and he kept informed about all the latest ideas. In the 1890s, many articles were written about a "New Age" of great passenger liners and what they might be like. He used these ideas to make his story more realistic and exciting.

Edward J. Smith, the proud captain of the doomed *Titanic*, was on his last trip as skipper. He went down with his ship.

THE DOOMED VOYAGE

...but what about the same names?

The *Titanic* was described as "the last word in luxury".

Robertson wanted a grand name — one that was suitable for the largest ship in the world. He used a name from Greek mythology, in which the Titans were ancient and powerful gods. The owners of the *Titanic* chose a name to give passengers a sense of strength and security.

19

...the shortage of lifeboats?

It was normal for ships to go to sea without enough lifeboats at this time. But the death toll on the *Titanic* led to a change in the law, and from then on there were always lifeboats for everyone.

...the collision with the iceberg?

Most sailors knew that icebergs drifted south into the shipping lanes of the North Atlantic in the Spring. It was a common danger. Robertson's invented ship, the *Titan*, was going so fast it reared out of the sea, slid on top of the iceberg and fell over. The *Titanic* was ripped open by the power of the ice. But the tragic results were the same...

HAUNTING LINKS

Blanche's Double Vision

On 10 April 1912 Blanche Marshall, her husband Jack and her family watched the Titanic leave Southampton, England. Suddenly, Blanche gripped Jack's arm and cried out:

"That ship is going to sink before it reaches America. Do something! You fools, I can see hundreds of people struggling in the icy water. Are you so blind that you're going to let them all drown?"

The Lusitania was torpedoed off the coast of Ireland by a German U-boat on 7 May 1915.

For five days the Marshall family tried to calm their mother down. They were stunned more than most people when the news broke that the *Titanic* had indeed sunk.

Three years later, the Marshalls were in New York. Jack booked return tickets on the Cunard liner *Lusitania* for 1 May. Blanche stared at the tickets with horror — and insisted that her husband change the reservation to another date. They caught an earlier ship and arrived home safely. The *Lusitania* became the first major civilian target of World War I: on 7 May, it was torpedoed by a German U-boat off the coast of Ireland with the loss of over 1,200 lives...

Captains and Crosses

In 1892 the English journalist William T. Stead had written a short story about an ocean liner that sank after hitting an iceberg in the Atlantic. His rescue ship was called the *Majestic*, and her captain was named E. J. Smith. In 1912, the unfortunate captain of the *Titanic* was also called E. J. Smith. And Stead was one of the passengers who drowned. When Stead sailed on the *Titanic*, he was carrying a crucifix. It was said to have appeared during a seance with Catherine the Great, Empress of Russia in the 18th century. This had brought bad luck to many people, but Stead *(below)* was keen to test its powers. In January 1912, he told a friend: " I have it now and I am curious to see whether any mischief will befall me ... Is it not thrilling?" He found his answer three months later.

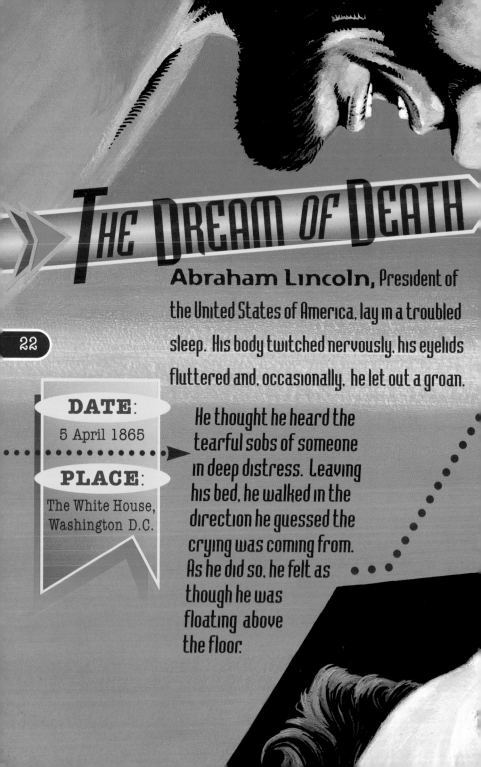

THE DREAM OF DEATH

Abraham Lincoln, President of the United States of America, lay in a troubled sleep. His body twitched nervously, his eyelids fluttered and, occasionally, he let out a groan.

DATE:
5 April 1865

PLACE:
The White House,
Washington D.C.

He thought he heard the tearful sobs of someone in deep distress. Leaving his bed, he walked in the direction he guessed the crying was coming from. As he did so, he felt as though he was floating above the floor.

Turning a corner,

he arrived at the large East Room. Peering in, he saw people filing past a raised platform, on which rested an open coffin. Women were holding handkerchiefs to their faces, and men bowed their heads. As if in slow motion, the President asked the nearest soldier why all these people were so upset. The soldier turned to face him and, with eyes that were brimming with tears, he replied: "It's the President, sir.

He's been killed by an assassin."

Lincoln's body turned to ice. He <u>must</u> look inside the coffin. Could it be true? He neared the coffin, afraid of what he might see. As he mounted the steps he gradually saw the bony outline of a face — <u>his</u> face! *He was staring at his own cold corpse. It was true ... he <u>was</u> dead!*

He threw his head back ... and with that movement he suddenly woke up. He lay still for a long time, almost afraid to move — just in case he really had died.

THE REALITY...

Lincoln was so troubled by the dream that he had to tell his wife and close friends about it. They assured him that he was a hero — that he had brought the terrible American Civil War to an end. And a grateful nation would not allow their leader to be murdered ...

15 April 1865

But the President could not shake the dream from his mind. Ten days later, on 15 April, in an attempt to help him relax, he visited *Ford's Theater* with his wife. He breathed a deep sigh of relief as the theatre lights dimmed and the play began. They were to be among the last breaths he took. As the lights were turned up near the end of the performance, the door to the box where the President sat was suddenly pushed open. A crazed supporter of the Confederate states, John Wilkes Booth, dashed in, raised a derringer pistol and shot the President in the back of the head from close range. Abraham Lincoln, who had survived four years of warfare, fell to the floor dead. He had been killed by an assassin's bullet ...just as the dream had foretold.

HISTORY BEHIND THE HAUNTING

For four long, bloody years the Northern and Southern states of the USA had been locked in a terrible civil war. The South had fought for the right to keep their black slaves, but the North wanted to see them freed. Cannons had thundered, rifles had cracked, and there had been fierce hand-to-hand fighting with sword and bayonet. Over half a million men had lost their lives. Abraham Lincoln, elected President at the beginning of the war, steered the Northern states to eventual victory. But peace did not bring an end to the hatred in the hearts of some Americans. John Wilkes Booth was part of a murderous conspiracy. He was injured jumping off the balcony of the theatre as he escaped, and he was later shot dead by police.

Flag of the Confederate South

Flag of the United States of America

25

HAUNTING EVIDENCE

The Power of Dreams

Scientists have proved that all of us dream, even if we can't remember much about it when we wake up. In 1952, investigations into sleep began after a scientist noticed that babies' eyes moved around under their eyelids while they slept. It was soon shown that these Rapid Eye Movements (REM) occurred when people were actually dreaming.

Everyone has between five and seven REM periods during the night — and dreams take up about one third of our sleeping time. This means that some 730 billion dreams are experienced each year in the USA alone!

HAUNTING ANSWERS

Can Dreams Foretell the Future?

Anxieties and worries are released when we fall asleep, and this can result in nightmares. Abraham Lincoln had been threatened by assassination many times. When he was elected President in 1860, he had to sneak into Washington at night, to be "sworn in" as leader of his country, for fear of being murdered. The South may have won the war if Lincoln had been killed then. It was only natural for such fears to be on his mind, and perhaps the terrible nightmare on 5 April 1865 was sending him a warning against such a danger.

SURRAT   BOOTH   HAROLD

War Department, Washington, April 20, 1865

$100,000 REWARD

THE MURDERER

Of our late beloved President,
Abraham Lincoln

IS STILL AT LARGE

$50,000 $25,000 $25,000

will be paid by this department for the apprehension of John Wilkes Booth.

will be paid by this department for the apprehension of Surrat

will be paid by this department for the apprehension of Harold

HAUNTING LINKS

Drawn to the World of Spirits

Mary Todd, Abraham Lincoln's wife, believed it was possible to contact the spirit world. Such people are called Spiritualists, and their beliefs were very popular in the second half of the 19th century. Her interest in "life after death" may have developed as a result of the death of her young son, William, whom she later tried to contact through seances and mediums.

Lincoln's White House Ghost

The first person to report seeing Abraham Lincoln's ghost was Grace Coolidge, wife of Calvin Coolidge, the 30th President of the United States. In the 1920s, Mrs Coolidge (*below*) said she saw Lincoln's face staring out of the window of the Oval Office at the White House.

When Queen Wilhelmina of the Netherlands stayed at the White House, in the 1930s, she claimed she heard a loud knock at the door. On opening it, she claimed, she was faced with the top hatted figure of Lincoln standing in the hallway. Queen Wilhelmina was also extremely interested in Spiritualism.

The Phantom Train

Lincoln's body was placed in a coffin on a train,
to be returned to his hometown of Springfield,
Illinois, for burial. People stood along the
railway tracks and the funeral train stopped
at each station for eight minutes, so that
Americans could pay their last respects.
Since that time, people have reported seeing a
phantom train pass along the same track —
and, as it does, clocks and watches are said to
stop for eight minutes. One carriage is said to
carry a band of skeleton musicians playing a
sad funeral march.

29

...clocks
are said
to stop
for
eight
minutes

THE LOST LEADER

General Sikorski was tired. Ever since his beloved Poland had fallen to the Nazis, he had worked constantly. As leader of the free Polish forces, he was needed everywhere. On 26 May he left England for a secret meeting in Cairo, the capital of Egypt, and back in London his office was quiet.

DATE: 26 May 1943

PLACE: Free Poland HQ, London

Suddenly the telephone bell rang.

"Hello?" Sikorski's secretary waited for a voice to respond. The reply was a little slow, as if it were coming from a great distance.

"General Sikorski's aeroplane has crashed at Gibraltar," the voice slowly informed the listener, in Polish. **"All passengers have perished!"**

"It can't be true!"

The secretary gasped in disbelief. *"Who is this?"* she demanded. But a click was all that could be heard as the voice vanished.

She rushed to one of Sikorski's officers and blurted out the news. "But it can't be true," he said. "We've just received a message that the General is safe. He's landed at Gibraltar for refuelling." The officer tried to reassure the secretary, and advised her to go back to her normal duties.

But the sinister phone calls kept on coming. Several more messages were received that day, all of them repeating the same news: *"The General has died in the plane crash."*

Eventually, after receiving further confirmation that the General was indeed safe, the calls were dismissed as the act of a crank who had the secret number of the headquarters.

General Sikorski's

staff did not inform him of the telephone calls. They reckoned that he had enough worries already.

Six weeks later, General Sikorski was on the return flight from his secret meeting at Cairo. The Liberator plane stopped at Gibraltar to be refuelled. After departing on 4 July, the plane suddenly plunged into the sea. While the pilot and a British officer survived, 15 other passengers died. Among them was General Sikorski.

Back at the free Polish London headquarters, the telephone rang. As usual, the secretary picked up the receiver.

"Hello?"

"I'm sorry to tell you that General Sikorski's plane has crashed," said the voice.

"All passengers have perished, except two." The secretary slumped back into her seat.

HISTORY BEHIND THE HAUNTING

In September 1939, Nazi Germany had invaded Poland. Britain and France warned Adolf Hitler, the leader of Germany, that if he did not withdraw then they would declare war. Germany ignored this ultimatum, and Europe was plunged into **a six-year conflict.**

Within six weeks Poland fell to the German Army, and in 1940 France was invaded and defeated. Many leaders of European countries fled to Britain, who still held out against the Germans. Among them was the leader of the free Polish forces, General Wladyslaw Sikorski.

The General was a difficult, stubborn man who had made many enemies — even among his own allies. He hated the Soviet Union, who suddenly became Britain's ally after being invaded by Germany in 1941.

The General was a difficult, stubborn man who had made many enemies...

HAUNTING EVIDENCE

Eerie Implications. . .

The British investigation of the crash revealed some strange details. The pilot of Sikorski's plane was experienced, yet he claimed that the control stick had jammed when he tried to gain height. The American makers of the Liberator, Mitchell, claimed that the kind of control fault described by the pilot was just not possible. In addition, the pilot was picked up in the water already wearing his life-jacket – when he didn't usually wear one.

Unidentified Passengers. . .

Observers saw another man, possibly the co-pilot, wearing a life-jacket after the plane had crashed. He climbed onto the wing before being washed away. Had the two airmen arranged to ditch the plane? Two of the passengers were known only as Mr Pinder and Mr Locke, and to this day nobody knows who they really were. Could they have been secret agents, hired to assassinate Sikorski?

Wartime Cargo. . .

Many goods were found among the wreckage, possibly smuggled from the Middle East. Britain was desperately short of ordinary foodstuffs as well as luxuries during the War, and the plane may have taken on tonnes of provisions at Gibraltar. Had too much baggage caused the aircraft to crash?

Despite all these odd details the investigation team decided that the crash was caused by a failure of the controls. The pilot was not blamed, and he continued to fly important people around for many years. . .

HAUNTING ANSWERS

THEORY 1 - Sikorski Assassinated

Winston Churchill, Britain's wartime Prime Minister, wanted to keep the powerful Soviet Union in the War. It's possible that promises about Polish territory had to be made to the Soviets — promises that Sikorski opposed. But many wanted him dead. So if Sikorski was assassinated, who killed him — the Russians, the British, the Germans. . .or, as the voice may suggest, the Poles themselves? But why ring up and confirm the deed?

35

THEORY 2 - Time Slip

Perhaps a shift in time had occurred — and the phone calls were echoes from the future. But there were some differences: for example, the first call had stated that all the passengers were dead, but the second explained that there were two survivors...

HAUNTING LINKS

Some people believe that it is possible for time to "slip". Distances and events suddenly collapse and come together, causing future events to become confused with what's happening in the present. The call about Sikorski's death may have slipped in time, giving a warning of events to come...

Cries From the Beach

On 19 August 1942 a massive commando raid took place on Nazi-occupied Dieppe, in northern France, by British and Canadian troops. It was a disaster, and many Allied soldiers lost their lives or were captured. During early August 1951, Mrs Dorothy Naughton and her sister-in-law were staying at the little coastal village of Puys, near Dieppe.

Around 4 a.m. Mrs Naughton was suddenly woken by the incredible noise of **gunfire and the whine of dive-bombers**. The sounds seemed to be coming from the beach. She woke her sister-in-law, and together they listened to the dull thud of explosions and the cries of injured men for almost *three hours*.

But nothing could be seen. It was as if they had mysteriously "slipped" into the Dieppe disaster of nine years before.

A VISION OF DEATH

During the early part of World War 2,
Wing Commander George Potter and Flying Officer Reg Lamb were drinking at a bar on an RAF bomber base in Egypt. Drinking with them were several other men, including a Wing Commander known as "Roy".

Roy had just been told a joke, and he threw his head back in laughter. As he did so, George Potter looked at him and had a frightening vision. He saw what he took to be the head and shoulders of the Wing Commander, swimming around in a blue-black pool. As he peered more closely, he saw that Roy's lips were drawn back, his flesh was peeling off — and his eyes were just empty, hollow sockets...

The next night, Roy flew off in his plane. Somewhere over the Mediterranean Sea, he was shot down. His aircraft burst into flames as it crashed into the water. The Wing Commander's body was not found for several days, by which time

the fish and the sea had ravaged his body, and his burnt flesh was peeling off...

THE PALACE OF GHOSTS

DATE:
10 August 1901

PLACE:
Versailles Palace,
near Paris

Eleanor Jourdain and Charlotte Moberly were like excited schoolgirls. This was their first visit to King Louis XIV's stunning and famous 17th-century Palace of Versailles.

Leaving the guided tour of the palace, the two ladies tried to find the private mansion retreat of Queen Marie-Antoinette, called Le Petit Trianon. This was tucked away somewhere in the huge grounds of the estate. Somehow, they missed the path and found themselves walking along a shady lane. Gradually, they were overcome with a dreadful feeling — as if something was very wrong. Trying to explain it afterwards, Eleanor Jourdain said: "I began to feel as if I were walking in my sleep. The heavy dreaminess was oppressive."

A stone cottage then came into view, and the two friends began to feel a little easier. At the door of the cottage, an older woman was handing a jug to a younger one — but their dresses belonged to a much earlier time. Confused, the English ladies asked directions from two men dressed in long green coats and three-cornered hats. They pointed out a path leading to a small circular platform that looked like a bandstand. On the steps slouched a male figure in a broad-brimmed hat, with **a heavy black cloak wrapped round his shoulders.**

Miss Jourdain recalled later: "At that moment the eerie feeling that had begun in the garden now turned to fear." Miss Moberly remembered that... "everything looked too unnatural. Even the trees seemed to have become flat and lifeless, as if they were a tapestry."

THE man on the steps turned to look at them, and Eleanor and Charlotte gasped. **His face was badly scarred** and pitted with the ravages of the smallpox disease. His face appeared "very evil and yet unseeing". They stood still, **frozen in their tracks,** until they were disturbed by the sound of footsteps running behind them… and another man came into view. He also wore a thick black cloak – clothing that struck the ladies as very odd for a hot August day. Waving his hands about, he called out that they **must not go towards the bandstand**…and instead resume their journey to Le Petit Trianon.

Crossing over a small wooden bridge, they glimpsed Marie-Antoinette's mansion *(below)*. But all the windows were shuttered.

On the terrace sat a young woman artist sketching the trees. The ladies could not see the entrance — until a man dressed as a footman beckoned to them.

As they entered the house, their disturbing sense of unease began to fall away. They joined a wedding party who were touring the mansion — and because the guests were dressed in the clothes of 1901, the two women began to feel more settled. At last, they had normal events happening around them in their own time — the "present".

The following year Eleanor and Charlotte returned to the scene of their fascinating adventure. To their astonishment, rusty gates blocked their path — and there was no trace of the stone cottage or wooden bandstand to be found...

Witnesses

Miss Charlotte Moberly was the principal of St. Hugh's College, Oxford, and Eleanor was the headteacher of a private school in London. When the two ladies compared experiences, they noticed certain differences. For example, Miss Jourdain had seen the cottage — but not the lady sketching the trees. In 1911, they published a book, entitled *An Adventure*, telling the story of **that fateful summer's day in August 1901...** in the hope that someone might provide an explanation.

Figures in 18th-century dress were also seen near Le Petit Trianon in 1910, 1938, 1949 and 1955...

42

HISTORY BEHIND THE HAUNTING

In 1789, France was rocked by revolution. Most of the nobles, and finally Louis XVI, were overthrown by the ordinary people. Particular hatred was directed against the King's Austrian-born wife, Marie-Antoinette, for her extravagant and lavish lifestyle. Eventually, both the King and the Queen were beheaded on the guillotine, together with thousands of French aristocrats.

43

HAUNTING EVIDENCE

The fact that the landscape had changed led the two women to believe that they had "stepped back in time" and met actual "living" people from more than 100 years in the past.

Old maps and paintings from the 18th century backed up their story. Believe it or not, Eleanor and Charlotte had seen and experienced the gardens in the way they were <u>originally</u> laid out, and this was something they could not possibly have known about...

HAUNTING ANSWERS

THEORY 1 - The Power of the Past

In the 1960s, a book called *The Trianon Adventure* suggested a possible explanation. Its author, Arnold O. Gibbons, believed that an image of the past can be so powerful that it makes itself appear again. The person who witnesses the image becomes convinced of its reality. When this trance-like state exists, everything in the present appears to vanish.

Gibbons identifies the running man who warned them away from the bandstand as Antoine Richard, head gardener at the Petit Trianon from 1765 to 1795. Many French revolutionaries wanted to destroy the elaborate palace gardens at Versailles, but Antoine persuaded them to save the gardens for the people of France. It could be that Antoine is the powerful link with the past.

THEORY 2 - The Power of Imagination

Psychologists believe that our imaginations can persuade us of a different reality. Perhaps, on that hot August day, the ladies' imaginations took over, convincing them that they had stepped through a "time gate".

THEORY 3 - You've Been Framed!

It's even been suggested that the two ladies stumbled across the making of a movie. But these were sensible, educated ladies! A more likely explanation is that they saw a rehearsal for a theatrical pageant in period costume.

HAUNTING LINKS

The Sword of Flame

In 1888, several witnesses at Varazdin, in northern Croatia, saw the amazing spectacle of infantry divisions marching **"through the skies".** They were led by a captain holding aloft a flaming sword. The figures kept reappearing over three days, and the vision lasted for several hours each time. But no historical connection was ever found between this "phantom army" and the area where it was seen . . .

🎯 THE GHOST SOLDIERS

apprentice youth learning a skill or trade

archaeologist person who digs up buildings and objects of people from the ancient past

deserted fled from the scene of fighting

Emperor leader of an empire

entrails inner organs of the body

identical exactly the same

legion a division of Roman forces; each legion had about 4,800 soldiers

livestock reared animals, including cattle and sheep

mutinied rebelled against their leaders

omens signs of the future

sacrifice killing of human or animal for religious reasons

🎯 THE DOOMED VOYAGE

catastrophe massive disaster

coincidence something happening in the same time or place but with no obvious connection

crucifix image of Christ on the cross, often worn round the neck

fate inevitable, unavoidable destiny

Jacobean style of the time of King James I (1603-25)

maiden voyage first commercial voyage of a ship

Parisian characteristic of Paris, capital of France

prophecy foretelling of the future

reservation booking a ticket in advance for a trip or event

seance ritual to communicate with the spirits of the dead

supernatural greater than normal, breaking the "laws of nature"

torpedo underwater missile fired at the hull of a ship

watertight compartments hull of a ship divided into sealed sections

🎯 THE DREAM OF DEATH

assassin person who murders for political reasons, named after a violent military and religious sect of Persia and Syria in the 11th-13th centuries

conspiracy secret plot

corpse body of a dead person

derringer small single-barrelled pistol named after gunsmith inventor Henry Derringer

medium person through whom spirits of the dead can communicate with the living

phantom ghost or spectre

White House official residence of the US Presidents, in Washington D.C.

seance ritual to communicate with the spirits of the dead

THE LOST LEADER

allies countries that have agreed to help each other in wartime

commando soldier specially trained for secret attacks on the enemy

echo sending back of sound by reflection

experienced having done something for many years

Gibraltar military base at the southern tip of Spain, under British control since 1704

Nazis paramilitary party of Adolf Hitler, who ruled Germany from 1933 to 1945

perished died or destroyed

provisions food, drink and general household items

Soviet Union nation of 15 states, dominated by Russia, that broke up in 1990

ultimatum final warning, with threat of action

Wing Commander RAF rank between Group Captain and Squadron Leader

THE PALACE OF GHOSTS

aristocracy titled members of the wealthy classes

bandstand structure for bands of musicians to play to an open-air audience

Croatia country of south-east Europe, on the east coast of the Adriatic Sea

deceived fooled, taken in

eerie spooky, unsettling

guillotine instrument of decapitation (beheading) used against the French aristocracy in the Revolution after 1791; it was invented by the politician and doctor Joseph Guillotin

mansion very large house, often called a château in France

oppressive feeling of being crushed, overpowered

pageant colourful show or procession marking scenes from history

phantom ghost or spectre

pitted marked with small holes

principal head teacher of private school or college

psychologist person who studies the human mind and behaviour

revolution attempt to overthrow a political system, usually by violent means

shutters wooden attachments to keep out heat in summer and cold in winter

smallpox highly infectious disease, not wiped out until the 1970s

tapestry ornamental, multi-coloured textile hung on walls

trance dazed, sleepy state

Index